I0417671

Where ...
Is Your Nearest Bear?

Andy Mason
Susie Maguire
Will Maguire

An Expect Magic Book

Well ... we talked about this Copyright page and what we should write on here and we decided to write this ...

We LOVED making this book.

We hope you LOVE it too.

We feel no crazy need to Copyright it and ...

we want you to feel free to share, share, share in whatever way makes you happy and in whatever way makes the world feel a little better, brighter and more full of love-liness.

ISBN: 978-1540590718

Dedications

Andy

This book is dedicated to everyone who loves bears …
which I think is everyone, because who doesn't love a bear?

Susie

Dedicated to my gorgeous son, who is my most favorite bear,
and to William Bear who traveled with me
and carried the magic.

Will

Dedicated to my lovely mummy, who has cared for me
all these years and Ted Bed Bear who
lets me sleep on his head.

About this book

This book was born in Andy's brain. We think that's because he loves the natural world, he loves bears and he loves creating songs and books that kids will love.

Andy knew the world was full of cool bears ... but ... he didn't know where they all lived, what they all ate and what made them similar and yet different. He also didn't know what made each of the species special.

This book answers all the questions he had about bears and ... you know what? Andy now knows that every species of bear is even cooler than he thought!

Furthermore, he now knows that his nearest bear is the North American Black Bear which can be found in New Mexico where he lives, as well as many other places across the US, Canada and Mexico.

We hope you enjoy this book and enjoy answering the question ...

Species of Bear: Polar Bear

Latin Name: Ursus Maritimus

Appearance:
Polar Bears are the biggest of the bears and are born with white fur that yellows with age.

An adult male Polar Bear weighs between 775 and 1300 lbs and females weigh about half that. The largest male Polar Bear EVER weighed 2209 lbs! That's as much as a small car! When they stand up a male bear can be as tall as 10 feet!

Polar Bears are born on land but spend much of their time on the sea ice. They have an amazing ability to swim and travel at sea and are even classified as Marine Mammals, putting them in the same category as whales, dolphins and seals.

Characteristics:
Polar Bears have large feet measuring up to 12 inches. This helps distribute their weight when on snow or thin ice, as well as being large paddles when they swim.

Polar Bears don't hibernate in the winter. They continue to hunt, unless it's extremely cold, then they may find a snow den. The exception is pregnant Polar Bears who go into a den for the colder months. They dig a small snow cave—just large enough for them to turn around in - and stay there for 4-8 months to give birth to their cubs.

Polar Bears sleep more during the day than at night because seals are more active at night. However, the idea of day and night mean little in the Arctic where there are 24 hours of light during summer and 24 hours of darkness in winter. Just like humans, Polar Bears sleep for seven to eight hours at a time. They also take naps to help conserve energy after hunting and eating.

Food:
The Polar Bear is the only absolute carnivore amongst all the bear species. They eat mostly ringed and bearded seals, although they do occasionally go swimming and catch fish to eat. They have also been photographed scaling near-vertical cliffs to eat birds, chicks and eggs!

Habitat:
Polar Bears live in the Arctic and are found in countries that ring the Arctic Circle: Canada, Russia, the United States (in Alaska), Greenland and Norway.

The largest population - 60% of Polar Bears - is in Canada.

Fun Fact:
A Polar Bear's skin is actually black. The color black is the best of all the colors for absorbing light and creating heat. This means the black skin of the Polar Bear helps to keep them warm.

Species: Brown Bear

Latin Name: Ursus Arctos

Subspecies:
Kodiak or Alaskan Brown Bear - Ursus Arctos Middendorffi
Grizzly Bear - Ursus Arctos Horribilis

Appearance:
Brown Bears are the second largest of the bear species and can weigh up to 850 lbs and can be as tall as 7 feet when standing.

They are called 'Brown' Bears but their fur color can range from very dark, almost black brown to a very light blond and can even be reddish/orange at times.

One of the ways to tell you are looking at a Brown Bear is that it has a very distinctive hump made of muscle on its shoulders.

Characteristics:
These giant bears tend to be solitary, except for females and their cubs, but there are times when they do gather together. For example, when the salmon swim upstream for summer spawning, dozens of bears may gather for a fish feast.

In the autumn, when preparing for winter hibernation they find a suitable cave or dig a den and they eat as much as 90 lbs of food each day. They weigh twice as much before hibernation as they do when they emerge in the spring.

Mama bears give birth during this winter hibernation, usually to a pair of cubs, while they are still sleeping!!!! Brown Bear cubs are born tiny and helpless. They nurse on their mother's milk until spring, staying with her for two to three years.

Food:
Brown Bears are omnivores and eat anything nutritious. Most of their diet is plant-based. They love berries, roots and grasses but they also eat insects and even meat if they find it. They also enjoy a fish feast whenever it's available.

Habitat:
Brown Bears live in more varied habitats than any other bear species and can be found in forests, mountains, tundra and even semi-desert areas.

They live in Europe, parts of Asia, Japan, western Canada and the United States, in Alaska, Idaho, Montana, Washington and Wyoming. They have the largest range of any bear species.

Fun Fact:
Despite being so big, Brown Bears are very fast and can run up to 30 miles per hour!

Species: American Black Bear

Latin Name: Ursus Americanus

Subspecies:
There are 16 subspecies of the American Black Bear, including:-
New Mexican Bear - Ursus Americanus Amblyceps
Kermode Bear or Spirit Bear - Ursus Americanus Kermodei
Glacier Bear - Ursus Americanus Emmonsii

Appearance:
The American Black Bear is the third largest of the bear species and although it is usually black with a tan muzzle, it can also have fur that is blue-gray, blue-black, whitish blue, brown, cinnamon, blonde or even white!

American Black Bears have straight faces and flat shoulders with rounded ears and a short tail. They can weigh up to 600 lbs and grow to be as tall as 7 feet when standing!

Characteristics:
The American Black Bear is very adaptable, intelligent and curious. It is also shy and generally avoids people and other confrontations.

American Black Bears hibernate for 6 or 7 months depending on their habitat and climate conditions. Some don't hibernate as long or even at all when food is abundant. They sleep in caves but they also make dens in lots of different places including open nests, fallen or hollow trees and even abandoned human buildings.

American Black Bears love to swim and they will cross ponds, lakes and rivers to get to better feeding grounds.

Food:
American Black Bears are eating machines. They eat field grasses, roots, tubers, nuts, berries of all kinds and fruits. They are also happy to eat ants, grubs, termites, beetles and other insects. Like Brown Bears, American Black Bears also like salmon and other kinds of fish and they will also hunt for small mammals.

Habitat:
American Black Bears are native to North America and can be found throughout the United States, Canada, and northern Mexico. They can be found in 41 of the 50 U.S. states and in all areas of Canada except … Prince Edward Island!

American Black Bears prefer to live in forests where there is a variety of food to eat and they can raise their cubs in relative peace.

Fun Fact:
The largest American Black Bear ever recorded weighed 880 pounds and lived in North Carolina. And … The American Black Bear population is estimated to be more than twice that of any other bear species!

Species: Asiatic Black Bear

Latin Name: Ursus Thibetanus

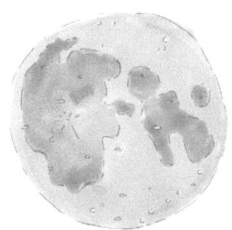

Subspecies:
There are several subspecies of the Asiatic Black Bear including:
Japanese Black Bear - Ursus Thibetanus Japonicus
Himalayan Black Bear - Ursus Thibetanus Laniger
Tibetan Black Bear - Ursus Thibetanus Thibetanus

Appearance:
The Asiatic Black Bear, also known as Moon Bear, are black with a light brown muzzle and a distinctive white patch on the chest in the shape of a V. They are medium sized bears and grow to be an average of 300 lbs and 5 feet in length.

They have long ears that stick out from the side of their head and powerful upper bodies for climbing trees.

Characteristics:
Asiatic Black Bears live in family groups of two adults and cubs from two litters.

They are good climbers of both rocks and trees and they climb to feed, rest, sunbathe, escape enemies and even hibernate. In fact, they spend half of their life in trees and are one of the largest arboreal mammals. They even create nests to make themselves comfortable!

They don't generally hibernate and even the ones that live in the colder northern areas tend to simply move south to warmer areas for winter rather than going to sleep. They are nocturnal animals that spend the day-time hours sleeping, coming out only under the cover of night to forage for food.

These bears are also noisy! They grunt, whine, roar, make slurping sounds and make a huge ruckus when they are hurt, scared or angry.

Food:
Asiatic Black Bears are omnivorous and will feed on insects, larvae, termites, grubs, carrion, bees, eggs, garbage, mushrooms, grasses, fruits, nuts, seeds, honey, herbs, acorns, grain and the occasional bird or rodent.

Habitat:
Asiatic Black Bears inhabit forested areas, especially hills and mountainous areas. They live throughout Southern Asia, Northeast China, Japan and Far Eastern Russia.

Fun Fact:
When they travel as a family, Asiatic Black Bears walk in order from largest to smallest.

Species: Spectacled Bear

Latin Name: Tremarctos Ornatus

Appearance:
The Spectacled Bear is a mid-sized bear that gets its name from the distinctive beige or ginger-colored markings across its face and upper chest. These markings make it look like the bears are wearing spectacles!

Overall, the Spectacled Bears fur is blackish in color, though some bears can have jet black, dark brown or even a reddish hue to their fur.

Males can weigh up to 340 lbs and can grow to a length of 5 feet.

These bears have a more rounded face than other bears and the shortest muzzle of all other living bears.

Characteristics:
Just like the Asiatic Black Bear, Spectacled Bears are 'arboreal' and spend a very great deal of their time in the trees. Once in a tree, they are known to build themselves platforms to help them hide, rest and even store food. Their excellent climbing ability allows them to climb even the tallest trees.

Spectacled Bears may be active during the day or night if they live in the mountains. Those that live in drier desert climates, are more likely to sleep during the day and forage at night.

Spectacled Bears are solitary and for the most part isolate themselves from other bears. However, like Brown Bears, they occasionally gather where there is a lot of available food.

These bears don't hibernate and are active year round.

Food:
Spectacled Bears are more herbivorous than most bears, with only 5% of their diet coming from meat. The most common foods for these bears include cactus, palm nuts, bamboo hearts, flower bulbs, fallen fruit from the forest floor and unopened palm leaves. They will also peel back tree bark to eat the nutritious second layer.

Habitat:
Spectacled Bears live in certain areas of northern and western South America. They are found in Venezuela, Colombia, Ecuador, Peru, western Bolivia, and northwestern Argentina. The species is found almost entirely in the Andes Mountains giving rise to their alternative name - the Andean Bear.

Fun Fact:
Paddington Bear, from the stories by Michael Bond, is a Spectacled Bear from "darkest Peru".

Species: Sloth Bear

Latin Name: Melursus Ursinus

Appearance:
Sloth Bears are distinctive looking bears with long shaggy coats, a shaggy mane, long sickle shaped claws and a specially adapted lower lip and palate designed for sucking up insects.

Their fur is generally dark brown/black with a yellowish/white muzzle and a whitish Y- or V-shaped mark on the chest.

Males can grow up to 6 feet tall when standing and weigh as much as 310 lbs while the females are smaller and weigh up to 210 lbs.

Characteristics:
Sloth Bears are nocturnal and make their day beds using broken branches in trees except in the wet season when they favor cozy caves. Unlike the Brown and Black Bears, Sloth bears do not hibernate.

Adult Sloth Bears travel in pairs and the males are notably gentle with the cubs. They are the only bear species to carry their cubs on their back.

Sloth bears are noisy, busy animals. They grunt and snort as they pull down branches to get fruit, dig for termites and ants, or snuffle under debris for grubs and beetles.

They walk in a slow, shambling way - slapping their feet down in a noisy, flapping way - but when they need to, they are capable of running faster than humans and though they appear slow and clumsy they are excellent climbers and climb to feed and rest - but when faced with an enemy they prefer to stand their ground.

Their long curved claws make it easy for them to access termite, ant and bee's nests.

Food:
Sloth Bears are insectivores and feed on termites (their favorites!), ants, honey-bee colonies and fruits.

Habitat:
Sloth bears live in a variety of dry and moist forests and in some tall grasslands, where boulders and scattered shrubs and trees provide shelter. Their range includes India, Sri Lanka and southern Nepal. They have also been spotted in Bhutan and Bangladesh.

Fun Fact:
Baloo from "The Jungle Book" by Rudyard Kipling is a Sloth Bear.

Species: Giant Panda (also known as Panda Bear or simply Panda)

Latin Name: Ailuropoda Melanoleuca

Appearance:
Giant Pandas are the most easily recognized bear with their distinctive black and white body fur and their black eyes and ears. Their Latin name literally translates to "black and white cat foot".

They are round and cuddly and very gentle looking too.

Adults grow to between 4 and 6 feet when standing, which is remarkable given that when they are born they are tiny and weigh less than 1/3 of a pound! They weigh between 200 and 250 lbs when fully grown.

Characteristics:
Pandas are solitary and shy creatures that prefer to live alone. Using their powerful sense of smell, Giant Pandas detect the scent of other Giant Pandas close by and avoid them. The only exception is during the breeding season (March to May) when males use their sense of smell to locate females.

With few natural predators, Giant Pandas are not picky when it comes to sleeping locations. They will fall asleep on the forest floor, cozying up next to a tree or balancing on a branch. Much of their time is spent eating, so Giant Pandas sleep for only 2–4 hours at a time.

Giant Pandas don't hibernate but instead migrate to lower elevations. The reason why Pandas don't hibernate is that they cannot stop eating. The low nutritional value of bamboo prevents them from building fat reserves to last them through the winter.

Food:
A Panda diet consists almost entirely of the leaves, stems and shoots of various bamboo species but they occasionally eat other grasses and even meat.

Oh and ... baby Pandas eat their mom's poop too! Ew!

Habitat:
Pandas live in large bamboo forests on humid and relatively high mountains and are only found in south central China.

Awesome Fact:
Pandas are no longer on the Endangered Species List! and FUN fact ... Pandas can poop up to 40 times a day!!!

Species: Sun Bear

Latin Name: Helarctos Malayanus

Appearance:
Sun Bears have sleek black/dark brown fur with an orange-yellow horseshoe shape on their chests.

The muzzle is short and light colored and in most cases the lighter area extends above the eyes.

They grow to about 4.5 feet and weigh up to 100 lbs.

Characteristics:
The shy Sun Bear, the smallest member of the bear family, lives a reclusive and insular life. They are the least known and the rarest of all the bear species.

Sun Bears are excellent climbers and spend considerable time in trees.

Because they live in tropical temperatures, Sun Bears do not need to hibernate and are able to mate at any time of year. Like Asiatic Black Bears and Sloth Bears, Sun Bears may hang out or live together while raising their cubs. Sun Bears will usually have two cubs at a time and care for them for two years until they are old enough to survive on their own.

Sun Bears have loose skin that allows them to twist when being bitten, giving them the ability to turn and bite their attacker. They also have very strong legs that are great for climbing. These characteristics help this bear protect itself from tigers and other large and dangerous predators that are common in their habitat.

Food:
Sun Bears eat lizards, small birds, rodents, insects, termites, fruit and most especially honey. Because of their voracious appetite for honey and honeycombs they are also known as "Honey Bears".

Habitat:
The Sun Bear can be found in the tropical rainforests of southeastern Asia, on the islands of Borneo and Sumatra, and in the forests of Malaysia, Thailand, Cambodia, Laos and Vietnam. There are also a few remote populations of Sun Bears in eastern India and southern China.

Fun Fact:
Sun Bears have VERY long tongues designed to let them scoop out honey from bee's nests and honeycombs.

Species: Koala Bear

Latin Name: Phascolarctos Cinereus

Appearance:
Koala Bears are small, cuddly, grey-furred, tree-dwellers. They have long curved claws that help them climb and cling to the trees where they live.

Koala Bears grow to be two to three feet long and weigh between 9 and 29 lbs.

Characteristics:
Koala Bears live in Eucalyptus trees. They love these trees so much, they rarely leave them.

Koala Bears are mostly nocturnal but these sleepy creatures doze, tucked into forks or nooks in the trees, between 18 and 22 hours per day. They have to sleep a lot because it takes lots of energy to digest the leaves they eat. When not asleep, a Koala Bear eats!

These bears communicate with each other by making a range of noises. The most startling and unexpected of these is a sound like a loud snore and then a belch, known as a 'bellow'.

Koala Bears are solitary animals that live alone throughout their lives except when raising their young.

Food:
Koala Bears only eat Eucalyptus leaves from Eucalyptus trees.

They eat a tremendous amount for their size—about two and a half pounds of leaves a day! They even store snacks of leaves in pouches in their cheeks.

These bears eat so many of these leaves that they take on the distinctive odor of Eucalyptus oil, which makes them smell like cough drops.

Habitat:
Koala Bears are only found in eastern and southeastern Australia where Eucalyptus forests and trees are abundant.

Fun Fact:
This cuddly animal is not a bear! It's also not cuddly.

It is a marsupial, or pouched mammal. After giving birth, a female Koala Bear carries her baby in her pouch for six months. When the infant emerges, it rides on its mother's back or clings to her belly, accompanying her everywhere until it is about a year old.

Species: Ted Bed Bear

Latin Name: Tedurlectus Ursa

Appearance:
Ted Bed Bear is very small, just 1 foot tall and weighs less than 10 lbs. He has grey fur with a very pleasing texture, a brown nose and a spot on one of his paws.

He has small eyes, a short tail, beige inner ears and no claws.

Characteristics:
Ted Bed Bear is extremely intelligent and a wonderful conversationalist.

He also has great patience and fortitude and is never happier than when being cuddled and used as a pillow.

His once white fur is now grey and can best be described as "scrumpled", a sure and certain sign of having been greatly loved.

The most faithful of friends, Ted Bed Bear can always be counted on to be there when you need him.

He also has the best, most crazy dreams that he shares in hilarious stories most mornings!

Food:
Ted Bed Bear survives entirely on LOVE!

Habitat:
Ted Bed Bear has travelled the world over, but wherever he is, his most favorite place is bed!!

Fun Fact:
Ted Bed Bear is openly sentient and hopes that one day, all Teddy Bears will be recognised as the living beings that they are.

Where ... is your nearest bear?

Cool facts about Bears in general

Now that we've had a look at all the different types of Bear species and learned what's unique about them, here's a list of some cool things that most Bears have in common:

- Bears are really smart. They have big brains, amazing memories and excellent navigation skills.
- Bears really care about their families and will even risk their lives to protect a cub or a sibling. When a member of a Bear family dies, they grieve for them as humans do.
- Bears have awesome senses of smell, sight and hearing. They can smell food, mates, cubs or predators from miles away! Wow!
- Bears have long been honored and revered as symbols of not only power and strength but also ... love.
- Many early civilizations told stories that became legends about the strength and protectiveness of bears.
- Like human children, bear cubs are extremely playful.
- Bears are found on every continent except Africa, Australia and Antarctica.
- Bears are mammals - just like humans.
- Bears are mostly solitary and actually quite docile. They have a bad reputation because they can become aggressive if they or their cubs are threatened, but in truth they are smart and shy and prefer to hide and avoid confrontation.
- Not all bears hibernate, but those that do can sleep for up to seven months.
- Bears don't pee or poop when they're hibernating!
- Bears are omnivores - just like humans - this means they eat both plants, animals and insects. Polar Bears are the exception, they are pure carnivores.
- Female Bears have their cubs between the age of 3 and 8.
- Bear cubs are born helpless. They are very small, weighing only about one pound and they have no teeth and cannot see. Cubs are very dependent on their mothers and are known to cry if separated from them.
- Cubs stay with their mothers until they are one and a half to two years old and then they will head off on their own.
- Some bears give birth while hibernating! In other words ... while they sleep!
- Bears walk flat footed, which allows them to walk upright, just like us.
- The main predator that bears have to worry about is, sadly, humans.

Andy Mason lives in Santa Fe, NM with his wife Anne
and their two children.

When he's not singing or reading books to kids, Andy
likes to watch sports and eat pizza.

Susie and Will live in Surrey, England with their two
bears (Ted Bed Bear and William Bear)
and The Queen.

They love travel and adventure, books, movies and
playing silly card games.

www.ingramcontent.com/pod-product-compliance
Lightning Source LLC
Chambersburg PA
CBHW050921290526
45792CB00002B/840